Baseball Stadium
Bucket List Journal

©2015 by Wandering Walks of Wonder Publishing

Printed in the United States of America

The Publisher: Wandering Walks of Wonder Publishing

Kansas City, MO 64118

USA

Website: www.wanderingwalksofwonder.com

ISBN-13: 978-1517397616

ISBN-10: 1517397618

This Journal

Belongs to:

_____

This exploration journal is a way to track your progress as you visit all major, minor, and independent league baseball stadiums across the US and Canada.

Professional baseball is played in over 250 ballparks in 47 states, 4 Canadian provinces and the District of Columbia. There currently are 30 Major League Ballparks, 159 Minor League Ballparks, 54 Independent League Ballparks and 14 Spring-Training Only Ballparks.

Major League Baseball is America's pastime and the easiest sport to get to check off those most wanted stadiums on your bucket list. This is because every team plays a huge number of games over six months, every week and nearly every day from April until October. Whether by air and/or car, this allows the possibility to see seven games in seven cities within a week.

Stadium Location Map

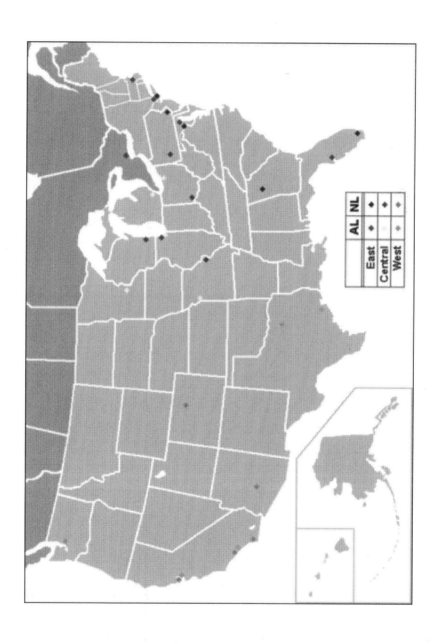

Stadium Name:		Date:

City/State:

Home Team Name:	Visiting Team Name:

Weather:	Seat Number and Location

Temperature:_____

	1	2	3	4	5	6	7	8	9	10		R	H	E
Visitors														
Home														

Winning Pitcher_____   Losing Pitcher_____

Stadium Description
_____
_____
_____
_____
_____

What did you enjoy most about the stadium?

_____

_____

_____

_____

_____

_____

What was the most memorable part of the game?

_____

_____

_____

_____

_____

Did the ballpark have a signature food or drink? How was it?

_____

_____

_____

_____

_____

How were the fans?

_____

_____

_____

_____

_____

_____

How was the in-game entertainment?
(Announcer, Music, mascots, fun events)

_____

_____

_____

_____

_____

What other sites did you see in the city during
your visit?

_____

_____

_____

_____

_____

Record other thoughts about the stadium or
tape your game ticket here.

Stadium Name:		Date:
City/State:		
Home Team Name:	Visiting Team Name:	

Weather:

Temperature:_____

Seat Number and Location

	1	2	3	4	5	6	7	8	9	10		R	H	E
Visitors														
Home														

Winning Pitcher_____   Losing Pitcher_____

Stadium Description

_____

_____

_____

_____

_____

_____

What did you enjoy most about the stadium?

_____

_____

_____

_____

_____

_____

What was the most memorable part of the game?

_____

_____

_____

_____

_____

Did the ballpark have a signature food or drink? How was it?

_____

_____

_____

_____

_____

What were the fans like?

_____

_____

_____

_____

_____

_____

How was the in-game entertainment?
(Announcer, Music, mascots, fun events)

_____

_____

_____

_____

_____

What other sites did you see in the city during
your visit?

_____

_____

_____

_____

_____

Record other thoughts about the stadium or tape your game ticket here.

Stadium Name:	Date:

City/State:

Home Team Name:	Visiting Team Name:

Weather:	Seat Number and Location

Temperature:_____

	1	2	3	4	5	6	7	8	9	10		R	H	E
Visitors														
Home														

Winning Pitcher_____   Losing Pitcher_____

Stadium Description

_____
_____
_____
_____
_____
_____

What did you enjoy most about the stadium?

_____

_____

_____

_____

_____

What was the most memorable part of the game?

_____

_____

_____

_____

_____

Did the ballpark have a signature food or drink? How was it?

_____

_____

_____

_____

_____

What were the fans like?

_____

_____

_____

_____

_____

How was the in-game entertainment?
(Announcer, Music, mascots, fun events)

_____

_____

_____

_____

_____

What other sites did you see in the city during
your visit?

_____

_____

_____

_____

_____

Record other thoughts about the stadium or tape your game ticket here.

_____

_____

_____

_____

_____

_____

_____

_____

_____

_____

_____

_____

_____

_____

_____

_____

_____

_____

_____

_____

_____

	Stadium Name:	Date:

City/State:

Home Team Name:	Visiting Team Name:

Weather:	Seat Number and Location

Temperature:_____

	1	2	3	4	5	6	7	8	9	10		R	H	E
Visitors														
Home														

Winning Pitcher_____   Losing Pitcher_____

Stadium Description

_____

_____

_____

_____

_____

_____

What did you enjoy most about the stadium?

_____

_____

_____

_____

_____

What was the most memorable part of the game?

_____

_____

_____

_____

_____

Did the ballpark have a signature food or drink? How was it?

_____

_____

_____

_____

_____

What were the fans like?

_____

_____

_____

_____

_____

_____

How was the in-game entertainment?
(Announcer, Music, mascots, fun events)

_____

_____

_____

_____

_____

What other sites did you see in the city during
your visit?

_____

_____

_____

_____

_____

Record other thoughts about the stadium or tape your game ticket here.

Stadium Name:	Date:
City/State:	

Home Team Name:	Visiting Team Name:

Weather:	Seat Number and Location

Temperature:_____

	1	2	3	4	5	6	7	8	9	10		R	H	E
Visitors														
Home														

Winning Pitcher_____   Losing Pitcher_____

Stadium Description
_____
_____
_____
_____
_____
_____

What did you enjoy most about the stadium?

_____
_____
_____
_____
_____

What was the most memorable part of the game?

_____
_____
_____
_____
_____

Did the ballpark have a signature food or drink? How was it?

_____
_____
_____
_____
_____

What were the fans like?

_____

_____

_____

_____

_____

How was the in-game entertainment?
(Announcer, Music, mascots, fun events)

_____

_____

_____

_____

_____

What other sites did you see in the city during
your visit?

_____

_____

_____

_____

_____

Record other thoughts about the stadium or tape your game ticket here.

	Stadium Name:	Date:

City/State:

Home Team Name:	Visiting Team Name:

Weather:	Seat Number and Location

Temperature:_____

	1	2	3	4	5	6	7	8	9	10		R	H	E
Visitors														
Home														

Winning Pitcher_____   Losing Pitcher_____

Stadium Description

What did you enjoy most about the stadium?

_____

_____

_____

_____

_____

What was the most memorable part of the game?

_____

_____

_____

_____

_____

Did the ballpark have a signature food or drink? How was it?

_____

_____

_____

_____

_____

How were the fans?

_____

_____

_____

_____

_____

_____

How was the in-game entertainment?
(Announcer, Music, mascots, fun events)

_____

_____

_____

_____

_____

What other sites did you see in the city during
your visit?

_____

_____

_____

_____

_____

_____

Record other thoughts about the stadium or tape your game ticket here.

Stadium Name:	Date:

City/State:

Home Team Name:	Visiting Team Name:

Weather:	Seat Number and Location

Temperature:_____

	1	2	3	4	5	6	7	8	9	10		R	H	E
Visitors														
Home														

Winning Pitcher_____   Losing Pitcher_____

Stadium Description

_____

_____

_____

_____

_____

_____

What did you enjoy most about the stadium?

_____

_____

_____

_____

_____

What was the most memorable part of the game?

_____

_____

_____

_____

_____

Did the ballpark have a signature food or drink? How was it?

_____

_____

_____

_____

_____

How were the fans?

_____

_____

_____

_____

_____

_____

How was the in-game entertainment?
(Announcer, Music, mascots, fun events)

_____

_____

_____

_____

_____

_____

What other sites did you see in the city during
your visit?

_____

_____

_____

_____

_____

_____

Record other thoughts about the stadium or
tape your game ticket here.

Stadium Name:	Date:

City/State:

Home Team Name:	Visiting Team Name:

Weather:	Seat Number and Location

Temperature:_____

	1	2	3	4	5	6	7	8	9	10		R	H	E
Visitors														
Home														

Winning Pitcher_____   Losing Pitcher_____

Stadium Description

_____

_____

_____

_____

_____

_____

What did you enjoy most about the stadium?

_____

_____

_____

_____

_____

What was the most memorable part of the game?

_____

_____

_____

_____

_____

Did the ballpark have a signature food or drink? How was it?

_____

_____

_____

_____

_____

How were the fans?

_____

_____

_____

_____

_____

_____

How was the in-game entertainment?
(Announcer, Music, mascots, fun events)

_____

_____

_____

_____

_____

_____

What other sites did you see in the city during
your visit?

_____

_____

_____

_____

_____

_____

Record other thoughts about the stadium or tape your game ticket here.

_____

_____

_____

_____

_____

_____

_____

_____

_____

_____

_____

_____

_____

_____

_____

_____

_____

_____

_____

_____

Stadium Name:	Date:

City/State:

Home Team Name:	Visiting Team Name:

Weather:	Seat Number and Location

Temperature:_____

	1	2	3	4	5	6	7	8	9	10		R	H	E
Visitors														
Home														

Winning Pitcher_____ Losing Pitcher_____

Stadium Description

_____

_____

_____

_____

_____

_____

What did you enjoy most about the stadium?

_____

_____

_____

_____

_____

_____

What was the most memorable part of the game?

_____

_____

_____

_____

_____

Did the ballpark have a signature food or drink? How was it?

_____

_____

_____

_____

_____

_____

How were the fans?

_____

_____

_____

_____

_____

_____

How was the in-game entertainment?
(Announcer, Music, mascots, fun events)

_____

_____

_____

_____

_____

What other sites did you see in the city during
your visit?

_____

_____

_____

_____

_____

_____

Record other thoughts about the stadium or tape your game ticket here.

_____

_____

_____

_____

_____

_____

_____

_____

_____

_____

_____

_____

_____

_____

_____

_____

_____

_____

_____

_____

_____

Stadium Name:	Date:

City/State:

Home Team Name:	Visiting Team Name:

Weather:	Seat Number and Location

Temperature:_____

	1	2	3	4	5	6	7	8	9	10		R	H	E
Visitors														
Home														

Winning Pitcher_____   Losing Pitcher_____

Stadium Description

_____
_____
_____
_____
_____
_____

What did you enjoy most about the stadium?

_____

_____

_____

_____

_____

_____

What was the most memorable part of the game?

_____

_____

_____

_____

_____

Did the ballpark have a signature food or drink? How was it?

_____

_____

_____

_____

_____

How were the fans?

_____

_____

_____

_____

_____

How was the in-game entertainment?
(Announcer, Music, mascots, fun events)

_____

_____

_____

_____

_____

What other sites did you see in the city during
your visit?

_____

_____

_____

_____

_____

Record other thoughts about the stadium or tape your game ticket here.

_____

_____

_____

_____

_____

_____

_____

_____

_____

_____

_____

_____

_____

_____

_____

_____

_____

_____

_____

_____

_____

Stadium Name:	Date:

City/State:

Home Team Name:	Visiting Team Name:

Weather:	Seat Number and Location

Temperature:_____

	1	2	3	4	5	6	7	8	9	10		R	H	E
Visitors														
Home														

Winning Pitcher_____   Losing Pitcher_____

Stadium Description

_____

_____

_____

_____

_____

_____

What did you enjoy most about the stadium?

_____

_____

_____

_____

_____

_____

What was the most memorable part of the game?

_____

_____

_____

_____

_____

_____

Did the ballpark have a signature food or drink? How was it?

_____

_____

_____

_____

_____

_____

How were the fans?

_____

_____

_____

_____

_____

_____

How was the in-game entertainment?
(Announcer, Music, mascots, fun events)

_____

_____

_____

_____

_____

_____

What other sites did you see in the city during
your visit?

_____

_____

_____

_____

_____

Record other thoughts about the stadium or tape your game ticket here.

Stadium Name:	Date:

City/State:

Home Team Name:	Visiting Team Name:
Weather:	Seat Number and Location

Temperature:_____

	1	2	3	4	5	6	7	8	9	10		R	H	E
Visitors														
Home														

Winning Pitcher_____   Losing Pitcher_____

Stadium Description

_____

_____

_____

_____

_____

_____

What did you enjoy most about the stadium?

_____

_____

_____

_____

_____

_____

What was the most memorable part of the game?

_____

_____

_____

_____

_____

_____

Did the ballpark have a signature food or drink? How was it?

_____

_____

_____

_____

_____

_____

How were the fans?

_____

_____

_____

_____

_____

_____

How was the in-game entertainment?
(Announcer, Music, mascots, fun events)

_____

_____

_____

_____

_____

What other sites did you see in the city during
your visit?

_____

_____

_____

_____

_____

Record other thoughts about the stadium or tape your game ticket here.

Stadium Name:	Date:

City/State:

Home Team Name:	Visiting Team Name:

Weather:	Seat Number and Location

Temperature:_____

	1	2	3	4	5	6	7	8	9	10		R	H	E
Visitors														
Home														

Winning Pitcher_____   Losing Pitcher_____

Stadium Description

_____

_____

_____

_____

_____

_____

What did you enjoy most about the stadium?

_____

_____

_____

_____

_____

_____

What was the most memorable part of the game?

_____

_____

_____

_____

_____

Did the ballpark have a signature food or drink? How was it?

_____

_____

_____

_____

_____

_____

How were the fans?

_____

_____

_____

_____

_____

_____

How was the in-game entertainment?
(Announcer, Music, mascots, fun events)

_____

_____

_____

_____

_____

What other sites did you see in the city during
your visit?

_____

_____

_____

_____

_____

Record other thoughts about the stadium or
tape your game ticket here.

Stadium Name:	Date:

City/State:

Home Team Name:	Visiting Team Name:

Weather:	Seat Number and Location
Temperature:_____	

	1	2	3	4	5	6	7	8	9	10		R	H	E
Visitors														
Home														

Winning Pitcher_____   Losing Pitcher_____

Stadium Description

What did you enjoy most about the stadium?

_____

_____

_____

_____

_____

_____

What was the most memorable part of the game?

_____

_____

_____

_____

_____

Did the ballpark have a signature food or drink? How was it?

_____

_____

_____

_____

_____

How were the fans?

_____

_____

_____

_____

_____

_____

How was the in-game entertainment?
(Announcer, Music, mascots, fun events)

_____

_____

_____

_____

_____

What other sites did you see in the city during
your visit?

_____

_____

_____

_____

_____

_____

Record other thoughts about the stadium or tape your game ticket here.

Stadium Name:	Date:

City/State:

Home Team Name:	Visiting Team Name:

Weather:	Seat Number and Location
Temperature:_____	

	1	2	3	4	5	6	7	8	9	10		R	H	E
Visitors														
Home														

Winning Pitcher_____   Losing Pitcher_____

Stadium Description

_____

_____

_____

_____

_____

_____

What did you enjoy most about the stadium?

_____

_____

_____

_____

_____

_____

What was the most memorable part of the game?

_____

_____

_____

_____

_____

Did the ballpark have a signature food or drink? How was it?

_____

_____

_____

_____

_____

How were the fans?

_____

_____

_____

_____

_____

_____

How was the in-game entertainment?
(Announcer, Music, mascots, fun events)

_____

_____

_____

_____

_____

What other sites did you see in the city during
your visit?

_____

_____

_____

_____

_____

Record other thoughts about the stadium or tape your game ticket here.

Stadium Name:	Date:

City/State:

Home Team Name:	Visiting Team Name:

Weather:	Seat Number and Location
Temperature:_____	

	1	2	3	4	5	6	7	8	9	10		R	H	E
Visitors														
Home														

Winning Pitcher_____   Losing Pitcher_____

Stadium Description

_____

_____

_____

_____

_____

What did you enjoy most about the stadium?

_____

_____

_____

_____

_____

_____

What was the most memorable part of the game?

_____

_____

_____

_____

_____

_____

Did the ballpark have a signature food or drink? How was it?

_____

_____

_____

_____

_____

_____

How were the fans?

_____

_____

_____

_____

_____

_____

How was the in-game entertainment?
(Announcer, Music, mascots, fun events)

_____

_____

_____

_____

_____

What other sites did you see in the city during
your visit?

_____

_____

_____

_____

_____

Record other thoughts about the stadium or tape your game ticket here.

Stadium Name:	Date:

City/State:

Home Team Name:	Visiting Team Name:

Weather:	Seat Number and Location

Temperature:_____

	1	2	3	4	5	6	7	8	9	10		R	H	E
Visitors														
Home														

Winning Pitcher_____   Losing Pitcher_____

Stadium Description

_____

_____

_____

_____

_____

What did you enjoy most about the stadium?

_____

_____

_____

_____

_____

_____

What was the most memorable part of the game?

_____

_____

_____

_____

_____

Did the ballpark have a signature food or drink? How was it?

_____

_____

_____

_____

_____

How were the fans?

_____

_____

_____

_____

_____

_____

How was the in-game entertainment?
(Announcer, Music, mascots, fun events)

_____

_____

_____

_____

_____

What other sites did you see in the city during
your visit?

_____

_____

_____

_____

_____

Record other thoughts about the stadium or
tape your game ticket here.

Stadium Name:		Date:

City/State:

Home Team Name:	Visiting Team Name:

Weather:	Seat Number and Location

Temperature:_____

	1	2	3	4	5	6	7	8	9	10		R	H	E
Visitors														
Home														

Winning Pitcher_____   Losing Pitcher_____

Stadium Description

_____

_____

_____

_____

_____

_____

What did you enjoy most about the stadium?

_____

_____

_____

_____

_____

_____

What was the most memorable part of the game?

_____

_____

_____

_____

_____

Did the ballpark have a signature food or drink? How was it?

_____

_____

_____

_____

_____

How were the fans?

_____

_____

_____

_____

_____

_____

How was the in-game entertainment?
(Announcer, Music, mascots, fun events)

_____

_____

_____

_____

_____

What other sites did you see in the city during
your visit?

_____

_____

_____

_____

_____

Record other thoughts about the stadium or
tape your game ticket here.

Stadium Name:	Date:

City/State:

Home Team Name:	Visiting Team Name:

Weather:	Seat Number and Location

Temperature:_____

	1	2	3	4	5	6	7	8	9	10		R	H	E
Visitors														
Home														

Winning Pitcher_____   Losing Pitcher_____

Stadium Description

What did you enjoy most about the stadium?

_____

_____

_____

_____

_____

_____

What was the most memorable part of the game?

_____

_____

_____

_____

_____

Did the ballpark have a signature food or drink? How was it?

_____

_____

_____

_____

_____

_____

How were the fans?

_____

_____

_____

_____

_____

_____

How was the in-game entertainment?
(Announcer, Music, mascots, fun events)

_____

_____

_____

_____

_____

What other sites did you see in the city during
your visit?

_____

_____

_____

_____

_____

Record other thoughts about the stadium or
tape your game ticket here.

Stadium Name:		Date:

City/State:

Home Team Name:	Visiting Team Name:

Weather:	Seat Number and Location

Temperature:_____

	1	2	3	4	5	6	7	8	9	10		R	H	E
Visitors														
Home														

Winning Pitcher_____   Losing Pitcher_____

Stadium Description
_____
_____
_____
_____
_____
_____

What did you enjoy most about the stadium?

_____

_____

_____

_____

_____

_____

What was the most memorable part of the game?

_____

_____

_____

_____

_____

Did the ballpark have a signature food or drink? How was it?

_____

_____

_____

_____

_____

How were the fans?

_____

_____

_____

_____

_____

_____

How was the in-game entertainment?
(Announcer, Music, mascots, fun events)

_____

_____

_____

_____

_____

_____

What other sites did you see in the city during
your visit?

_____

_____

_____

_____

_____

_____

Record other thoughts about the stadium or tape your game ticket here.

Stadium Name:		Date:
City/State:		
Home Team Name:	Visiting Team Name:	

Weather:

Temperature:_____

Seat Number and Location

_____

	1	2	3	4	5	6	7	8	9	10		R	H	E
Visitors														
Home														

Winning Pitcher_____   Losing Pitcher_____

Stadium Description

_____

_____

_____

_____

_____

_____

What did you enjoy most about the stadium?

_____
_____
_____
_____
_____
_____

What was the most memorable part of the game?

_____
_____
_____
_____
_____
_____

Did the ballpark have a signature food or drink? How was it?

_____
_____
_____
_____
_____
_____

How were the fans?

_____

_____

_____

_____

_____

_____

How was the in-game entertainment?
(Announcer, Music, mascots, fun events)

_____

_____

_____

_____

_____

_____

What other sites did you see in the city during
your visit?

_____

_____

_____

_____

_____

_____

Record other thoughts about the stadium or tape your game ticket here.

_____

_____

_____

_____

_____

_____

_____

_____

_____

_____

_____

_____

_____

_____

_____

_____

_____

_____

Stadium Name:	Date:

City/State:

Home Team Name:	Visiting Team Name:

Weather:	Seat Number and Location

Temperature:_____

	1	2	3	4	5	6	7	8	9	10	R	H	E
Visitors													
Home													

Winning Pitcher_____   Losing Pitcher_____

Stadium Description

What did you enjoy most about the stadium?

_____

_____

_____

_____

_____

_____

What was the most memorable part of the game?

_____

_____

_____

_____

_____

Did the ballpark have a signature food or drink? How was it?

_____

_____

_____

_____

_____

How were the fans?

_____

_____

_____

_____

_____

_____

How was the in-game entertainment?
(Announcer, Music, mascots, fun events)

_____

_____

_____

_____

_____

_____

What other sites did you see in the city during
your visit?

_____

_____

_____

_____

_____

_____

Record other thoughts about the stadium or tape your game ticket here.

| Stadium Name: | Date: |

City/State:

| Home Team Name: | Visiting Team Name: |

| Weather: | Seat Number and Location |

Temperature:_____

	1	2	3	4	5	6	7	8	9	10		R	H	E
Visitors														
Home														

Winning Pitcher_____   Losing Pitcher_____

Stadium Description

_____

_____

_____

_____

_____

_____

What did you enjoy most about the stadium?

_____
_____
_____
_____
_____

What was the most memorable part of the game?

_____
_____
_____
_____
_____

Did the ballpark have a signature food or drink? How was it?

_____
_____
_____
_____
_____

How were the fans?

_____

_____

_____

_____

_____

How was the in-game entertainment?
(Announcer, Music, mascots, fun events)

_____

_____

_____

_____

_____

What other sites did you see in the city during
your visit?

_____

_____

_____

_____

_____

Record other thoughts about the stadium or tape your game ticket here.

Stadium Name:	Date:

City/State:

Home Team Name:	Visiting Team Name:

Weather:	Seat Number and Location

Temperature:_____

	1	2	3	4	5	6	7	8	9	10		R	H	E
Visitors														
Home														

Winning Pitcher_____   Losing Pitcher_____

Stadium Description
_____
_____
_____
_____
_____
_____

What did you enjoy most about the stadium?

_____
_____
_____
_____
_____
_____

What was the most memorable part of the game?

_____
_____
_____
_____
_____
_____

Did the ballpark have a signature food or drink? How was it?

_____
_____
_____
_____
_____
_____

How were the fans?

_____

_____

_____

_____

_____

_____

How was the in-game entertainment?
(Announcer, Music, mascots, fun events)

_____

_____

_____

_____

_____

What other sites did you see in the city during
your visit?

_____

_____

_____

_____

_____

Record other thoughts about the stadium or tape your game ticket here.

_____

_____

_____

_____

_____

_____

_____

_____

_____

_____

_____

_____

_____

_____

_____

_____

_____

_____

Stadium Name:	Date:

City/State:

Home Team Name:	Visiting Team Name:

Weather:	Seat Number and Location

Temperature:_____

	1	2	3	4	5	6	7	8	9	10		R	H	E
Visitors														
Home														

Winning Pitcher_____   Losing Pitcher_____

Stadium Description
_____
_____
_____
_____
_____
_____

What did you enjoy most about the stadium?

_____

_____

_____

_____

_____

What was the most memorable part of the game?

_____

_____

_____

_____

_____

Did the ballpark have a signature food or drink? How was it?

_____

_____

_____

_____

_____

How were the fans?

_____

_____

_____

_____

_____

_____

How was the in-game entertainment?
(Announcer, Music, mascots, fun events)

_____

_____

_____

_____

_____

What other sites did you see in the city during
your visit?

_____

_____

_____

_____

_____

Record other thoughts about the stadium or
tape your game ticket here.

Stadium Name:	Date:

City/State:

Home Team Name:	Visiting Team Name:

Weather:	Seat Number and Location
☀ ⛅ 🌧	
Temperature:_____	

	1	2	3	4	5	6	7	8	9	10		R	H	E
Visitors														
Home														

Winning Pitcher_____   Losing Pitcher_____

Stadium Description
_____
_____
_____
_____
_____
_____

What did you enjoy most about the stadium?

_____
_____
_____
_____
_____
_____

What was the most memorable part of the game?

_____
_____
_____
_____
_____
_____

Did the ballpark have a signature food or drink? How was it?

_____
_____
_____
_____
_____
_____

How were the fans?

_____

_____

_____

_____

_____

_____

How was the in-game entertainment?
(Announcer, Music, mascots, fun events)

_____

_____

_____

_____

_____

What other sites did you see in the city during
your visit?

_____

_____

_____

_____

_____

Record other thoughts about the stadium or tape your game ticket here.

Stadium Name:	Date:

City/State:

Home Team Name:	Visiting Team Name:

Weather:	Seat Number and Location

Temperature:_____

	1	2	3	4	5	6	7	8	9	10	R	H	E
Visitors													
Home													

Winning Pitcher_____   Losing Pitcher_____

Stadium Description

What did you enjoy most about the stadium?

_____
_____
_____
_____
_____
_____

What was the most memorable part of the game?

_____
_____
_____
_____
_____
_____

Did the ballpark have a signature food or drink? How was it?

_____
_____
_____
_____
_____
_____

How were the fans?

_____

_____

_____

_____

_____

How was the in-game entertainment?
(Announcer, Music, mascots, fun events)

_____

_____

_____

_____

_____

What other sites did you see in the city during
your visit?

_____

_____

_____

_____

_____

Record other thoughts about the stadium or
tape your game ticket here.

Stadium Name:		Date:
City/State:		
Home Team Name:	Visiting Team Name:	

Weather:	Seat Number and Location
☀ ⛅ 🌧 Temperature:_____	

	1	2	3	4	5	6	7	8	9	10		R	H	E
Visitors														
Home														

Winning Pitcher_____   Losing Pitcher_____

Stadium Description

_____

_____

_____

_____

_____

_____

What did you enjoy most about the stadium?

_____

_____

_____

_____

_____

What was the most memorable part of the game?

_____

_____

_____

_____

_____

Did the ballpark have a signature food or drink? How was it?

_____

_____

_____

_____

_____

How were the fans?

_____

_____

_____

_____

_____

How was the in-game entertainment?
(Announcer, Music, mascots, fun events)

_____

_____

_____

_____

_____

What other sites did you see in the city during
your visit?

_____

_____

_____

_____

_____

Record other thoughts about the stadium or
tape your game ticket here.

Stadium Name:	Date:

City/State:

Home Team Name:	Visiting Team Name:

Weather:	Seat Number and Location

Temperature:_____

	1	2	3	4	5	6	7	8	9	10		R	H	E
Visitors														
Home														

Winning Pitcher_____   Losing Pitcher_____

Stadium Description

What did you enjoy most about the stadium?

_____

_____

_____

_____

_____

_____

What was the most memorable part of the game?

_____

_____

_____

_____

_____

_____

Did the ballpark have a signature food or drink? How was it?

_____

_____

_____

_____

_____

_____

How were the fans?

_____

_____

_____

_____

_____

_____

How was the in-game entertainment?
(Announcer, Music, mascots, fun events)

_____

_____

_____

_____

_____

What other sites did you see in the city during
your visit?

_____

_____

_____

_____

_____

Record other thoughts about the stadium or
tape your game ticket here.

Stadium Name:	Date:

City/State:

Home Team Name:	Visiting Team Name:

Weather:	Seat Number and Location

Temperature:_____

	1	2	3	4	5	6	7	8	9	10		R	H	E
Visitors														
Home														

Winning Pitcher_____   Losing Pitcher_____

Stadium Description

_____

_____

_____

_____

_____

_____

What did you enjoy most about the stadium?

_____
_____
_____
_____
_____
_____

What was the most memorable part of the game?

_____
_____
_____
_____
_____
_____

Did the ballpark have a signature food or drink? How was it?

_____
_____
_____
_____
_____
_____

How were the fans?

_____

_____

_____

_____

_____

_____

How was the in-game entertainment?
(Announcer, Music, mascots, fun events)

_____

_____

_____

_____

_____

What other sites did you see in the city during
your visit?

_____

_____

_____

_____

_____

Record other thoughts about the stadium or tape your game ticket here.

		Stadium Name:									Date:		

Stadium Name:

Date:

City/State:

Home Team Name:

Visiting Team Name:

Weather:

Seat Number and Location

Temperature:_____

	1	2	3	4	5	6	7	8	9	10		R	H	E
Visitors														
Home														

Winning Pitcher_____   Losing Pitcher_____

Stadium Description

_____

_____

_____

_____

_____

_____

What did you enjoy most about the stadium?

_____

_____

_____

_____

_____

_____

What was the most memorable part of the game?

_____

_____

_____

_____

_____

_____

Did the ballpark have a signature food or drink? How was it?

_____

_____

_____

_____

_____

_____

How were the fans?

_____

_____

_____

_____

_____

_____

How was the in-game entertainment?
(Announcer, Music, mascots, fun events)

_____

_____

_____

_____

_____

What other sites did you see in the city during
your visit?

_____

_____

_____

_____

_____

_____

Record other thoughts about the stadium or tape your game ticket here.

Stadium Name:		Date:
City/State:		
Home Team Name:	Visiting Team Name:	

Weather:

Temperature:_____

Seat Number and Location

_____

	1	2	3	4	5	6	7	8	9	10		R	H	E
Visitors														
Home														

Winning Pitcher_____   Losing Pitcher_____

Stadium Description

_____

_____

_____

_____

_____

_____

What did you enjoy most about the stadium?

_____

_____

_____

_____

_____

_____

What was the most memorable part of the game?

_____

_____

_____

_____

_____

Did the ballpark have a signature food or drink? How was it?

_____

_____

_____

_____

_____

How were the fans?

_____

_____

_____

_____

_____

_____

How was the in-game entertainment?
(Announcer, Music, mascots, fun events)

_____

_____

_____

_____

_____

What other sites did you see in the city during
your visit?

_____

_____

_____

_____

_____

Record other thoughts about the stadium or tape your game ticket here.

_____

_____

_____

_____

_____

_____

_____

_____

_____

_____

_____

_____

_____

_____

_____

_____

_____

_____

Stadium Name:	Date:
City/State:	

Home Team Name:	Visiting Team Name:

Weather:	Seat Number and Location

Temperature:_____

	1	2	3	4	5	6	7	8	9	10		R	H	E
Visitors														
Home														

Winning Pitcher_____   Losing Pitcher_____

Stadium Description

_____
_____
_____
_____
_____
_____

What did you enjoy most about the stadium?

_____
_____
_____
_____
_____

What was the most memorable part of the game?

_____
_____
_____
_____
_____

Did the ballpark have a signature food or drink? How was it?

_____
_____
_____
_____
_____

How were the fans?

_____

_____

_____

_____

_____

_____

How was the in-game entertainment?
(Announcer, Music, mascots, fun events)

_____

_____

_____

_____

_____

What other sites did you see in the city during
your visit?

_____

_____

_____

_____

_____

Record other thoughts about the stadium or
tape your game ticket here.

_____

_____

_____

_____

_____

_____

_____

_____

_____

_____

_____

_____

_____

_____

_____

_____

_____

_____

_____

_____

_____

Stadium Name:	Date:
City/State:	

Home Team Name:	Visiting Team Name:

Weather:	Seat Number and Location
Temperature:_____	

	1	2	3	4	5	6	7	8	9	10		R	H	E
Visitors														
Home														

Winning Pitcher_____   Losing Pitcher_____

Stadium Description
_____
_____
_____
_____
_____
_____

What did you enjoy most about the stadium?

_____

_____

_____

_____

_____

What was the most memorable part of the game?

_____

_____

_____

_____

_____

Did the ballpark have a signature food or drink? How was it?

_____

_____

_____

_____

_____

How were the fans?

_____

_____

_____

_____

_____

_____

How was the in-game entertainment?
(Announcer, Music, mascots, fun events)

_____

_____

_____

_____

_____

What other sites did you see in the city during
your visit?

_____

_____

_____

_____

_____

_____

Record other thoughts about the stadium or
tape your game ticket here.

If you enjoyed this journal, we have many more styles and types to choose from. Visit our website for a complete list of journals.

www.wanderingwalksofwonder.com

Football Stadiums Journal

Bucket List Journal

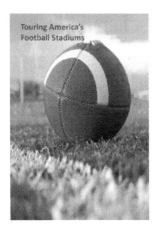

National Parks Journal

Lighthouse Exploration Journal

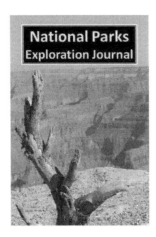

Made in the USA
Middletown, DE
12 May 2019